SPEAK UP!
CONFRONTING DISCRIMINATION IN YOUR DAILY LIFE™

CONFRONTING
DISCRIMINATION
AGAINST
IMMIGRANTS

CARLA MOONEY

Rosen
YA™
New York

Published in 2018 by The Rosen Publishing Group, Inc.
29 East 21st Street, New York, NY 10010

First Edition

Library of Congress Cataloging-in-Publication Data

Names: Mooney, Carla, 1970–author.
Title: Confronting discrimination against immigrants / Carla Mooney.
Description: New York: Rosen Publishing, 2018 | Series: Speak up! Confronting discrimination in your daily life | Includes bibliographical references and index. | Audience: Grades 7-12.
Identifiers: LCCN 2017015794| ISBN 9781538381670 (library bound) | ISBN 9781538381649 (pbk.) | ISBN 9781538381656 (6 pack)
Subjects: LCSH: Immigrants—United States—Social conditions—Juvenile literature. | Discrimination—United States—Juvenile literature. | Racism—United States—Juvenile literature. | United States–Race relations.
Classification: LCC E184.A1 M64 2018 | DDC 305.800973—dc23
LC record available at https://lccn.loc.gov/2017015794

Manufactured in China

CONTENTS

INTRODUCTION

Iraqi-born Israa and her mother moved to the United States when she was twelve years old to escape the violence of Syria's civil war. The young girl wondered what her new life in the United States would be like. She worried that she would not fit in with other kids. She also feared that people would hate her because she was Muslim and an immigrant. "At first I was scared that Americans are not [accepting] of our religion and our culture," she said in a March 2017 interview on Today.com. Now sixteen years old, Israa and her mother live in Pittsburgh, Pennsylvania, where she attends Allderdice High School. She admits she often hears stereotypes about her heritage. "It is true, I am a Muslim. It is true, I come from Iraq, but just because ten or five people are terrorists doesn't make the whole religion terrorist. We are not related to that at all. We're running from terror," Israa said. "So how are we terrorists?"

At school, Israa has found a support system in an after-school club, Global Minds. The club's founder, fifteen-year-old Peyton Klein, started Global Minds as a way to counter intolerance and discrimination against people of different ethnic backgrounds, immigrants, and refugees. Global Minds encourages American-born students to get to know and interact with foreign-born students who speak English as a second language (ESL). While they help each other with homework, club members also learn about human rights, diversity,

Peyton Klein, center, laughs with classmates from Syria and Saudi Arabia during Global Minds, a weekly after-school club she founded at their high school in Pittsburgh, Pennsylvania.

sustainable development, and international relations. The American-born students discover more about countries such as Syria and Mexico. "We get to see how similar we all are," said Ali Axtman, a sixteen-year-old student from Pittsburgh, in the interview. "When I think of Syria and Iraq, I don't just think of war-torn countries. I think of my friends." Klein believes that instead of fearing immigrants, American students can be their allies. She hopes to one day expand Global Minds to other schools nationwide.

For centuries, people have moved to new countries for many different reasons. Some are drawn by the promise of good jobs, higher wages, and a better quality of life. Others move to be closer to family or friends. Others are pushed to leave their home countries to escape political persecution, violence, and war. Some are forced to move because of natural disasters, such as flooding and famine.

The United States has the world's largest immigrant population, numbering forty-one million. In 2015 alone,

Many immigrants from nations around the world arrive in the United States through one of the country's busy international airports, such as Chicago's O'Hare Airport.

1.38 million foreign-born individuals moved to the United States, according to the Migration Policy Institute. Many of these immigrants came from India, China, Mexico, the Philippines, and Canada.

Americans' views on immigrants are mixed. According to a 2015 Pew Research Center poll, 41 percent of Americans said they believed immigrants are a burden because they take jobs, housing, and health care from native-born American citizens. In addition, the threat of terrorism has created a fear of immigrants from the Middle East and Muslim countries. According to a January 2017 Pew Research Center poll, 46 percent of Americans said that a large number of refugees from countries like Iraq and Syria were a major threat to US safety, while 35 percent considered the refugees to be a minor threat.

This anti-immigration sentiment has led to discrimination in many forms, from slurs and insults to employment bias and refusal of services. In some cases, discrimination can turn violent. In 2015, hate crimes rose 6 percent over 2014, driven by an increase in attacks against Muslims, according to a report by the Federal Bureau of Investigation (FBI).

In response to discrimination and violence against immigrants, young people like Peyton Klein are standing up and speaking out for the fair treatment of all people, regardless of where they or their parents were born. Said Klein, "It is such a relevant and pivotal moment. As students, we can conform to what is happening or we can rise up and make our students feel welcome and understood."

CHAPTER ONE

HISTORY OF DISCRIMINATION AGAINST IMMIGRANTS

Since its founding, the United States has been a destination for immigrants searching for a better life for themselves and their families. At the base of the Statue of Liberty, a plaque reads, "Give me your tired, your poor, your huddled masses yearning to breathe free." It stands as a symbol of welcome for immigrants from countries around the world coming to the United States. Since its foundation, immigrants have been making their homes in a wide variety of US states and communities.

The first large groups of immigrants came from northern and western Europe. In the 1850s, groups of Irish immigrants settled along the East Coast and in the southern states. In the 1880s, German immigrants became the largest immigrant group, settling in the Midwest and South. In the 1880s, Chinese immigrants were the largest foreign-born population in the western states. In the early 1900s, immigrants from southern and eastern Europe arrived in the United States. By the 1930s, Italians had become the largest immigrant group in the country. After 1965, the makeup of immigrants changed again. Mexicans became the country's largest immigrant group in thirty-three states by 2013.

The Statue of Liberty has stood as a symbol of welcome and inspiration for decades to immigrants sailing past her in New York Harbor as they arrive in New York City.

According to a 2015 study by the Pew Research Center, nearly 59 million immigrants have arrived in the United States in the past fifty years, making up a near-record 14 percent of the US population. The foreign-born population is defined as all people who were not US citizens at birth, including documented and undocumented immigrants. Since 1965, the majority of immigrants have arrived from Latin America (51 percent) and Asia (25 percent).

FACING DISCRIMINATION

Although they came to the United States to improve their lives, immigrants throughout history have found that settling into American communities has not always been easy. Many have faced discrimination at work, at school, and in the community. Discrimination involves treating people negatively because they look, sound, or dress differently or because they appear to be from another country or from a different ethnic background, even if they are not.

Many immigrants encounter discrimination in their daily lives. Often, this discrimination takes the form of microaggressions, which are everyday nonphysical slights, snubs, or insults. Whether intentional or unintentional, microaggressions send hostile, derogatory, or negative messages to a person based simply on their immigrant status. In many cases, these messages are meant to demean, threaten, and intimidate another person or treat them as if they are inferior. Microaggressions can be subtle. For example, a person who overly compliments an Asian immigrant for speaking English well may be sending a message that the immigrant is not a "true" American and will therefore always be a foreigner who does not fit in. Other microaggressions are more direct. For example, a person may try to pull at a Muslim woman's hijab, asking her what her hair looks like and whether she is forced to wear it.

DISCRIMINATION AT WORK

Many immigrants face discrimination in the workplace. Coworkers may intentionally and unintentionally give slights, snubs, or insults. Discrimination also occurs when employers make rules that require employees to speak English only or to dress a certain way. Not considering a person for a job because he or she has an accent or an ethnic appearance is also discrimination. For example, if an Indian woman is passed over for a job as a receptionist because the interviewer says she does not have an "all-American" front office appearance, that is an example of outright discrimination.

Many immigrants do not feel comfortable standing up for their rights, which can lead to some employers and others taking advantage of them. Recognizing the immigrants' desperation to keep their jobs, some employers pay them less and make them work in undesirable and even unsafe conditions. Undocumented immigrants in particular are targets for discrimination at work, as they are often reluctant to make complaints and may not be fluent in English. An undocumented immigrant living in Oklahoma, Ignacio says that he has lost more than $100,000 to fraud, as a supplier for his secondhand toy store took his money but failed to deliver a trailer full of merchandise. Afraid of being deported, Ignacio never reported it to the police.

HOUSING DISCRIMINATION

Immigrants also face discrimination when trying to find a safe, affordable place to live. Realtors may not show them all available apartments or homes for rent or sale. Landlords may charge immigrants increased rents and fees. Some landlords will take advantage of immigrant tenants. In Utah, one landlord knowingly

Two brothers play catch in the parking lot in front of their home in Colorado's San Luis Valley, in one of the country's largest migrant housing developments.

rented apartments infested with bedbugs to families of Myanmar refugees. If a family reported the bugs, the landlord charged them expensive fees to have the bugs removed. If they did not pay, the landlord threatened to have them evicted. Unable to speak English well and unfamiliar with their rights, many of the families agreed to the landlord's demands, even though they were being exploited.

UNDOCUMENTED IMMIGRANTS

While many immigrants enter and stay in the United States legally, some immigrants do not have a legal right to be and remain in the country. These people are called undocumented immigrants. According to the Pew Research Center, approximately 11.1 million undocumented immigrants lived in the United States in 2014, a number that has remained unchanged since 2009. A little over half of undocumented immigrants (52 percent) came from Mexico, while others came from other areas of the world, such as Asia, Central America, and Africa. In addition, the majority (66 percent) have lived in the United States for at least ten years. Although some undocumented immigrants enter the country illegally, a significant number entered the United States legally—either as tourists or on a temporary visa—and then did not leave. Because they do not have legal paperwork allowing them to stay in the United States, many undocumented immigrants live in fear that they will be discovered and deported.

Another example of discrimination against immigrants is when schools ignore the needs of immigrant students. It is discriminatory for service providers to require identification of both parents and children before processing requests for services or denying service requests entirely because of a parent's limited ability to speak English. When this happens, immigrant children or children of immigrants may have trouble accessing health care or necessary educational services.

WHAT CAUSES DISCRIMINATION AGAINST IMMIGRANTS?

Many times, discrimination against immigrants is fueled by racism. Immigrants from different parts of the world may look, sound, or dress differently from the majority of people in the communities where they live. Studies have found that immigrants with darker skin and thicker accents are more likely to experience discrimination than light-skinned, English-speaking immigrants. According to a 2015 report by the Migration Policy Institute, darker-skinned Latino immigrants are more likely to earn lower wages and be stopped by the police than lighter-skinned Latino immigrants.

Discrimination against immigrants is also caused by fear. Many people fear that an influx of new workers into the economy will cause them to lose their jobs and their ability to support their families. According to a 2014 Reuters/Ipsos poll, 70 percent of Americans said undocumented immigrants threatened traditional American beliefs and customs and jeopardized the US economy. Others feared for their personal or national safety after terrorist attacks in San Bernardino, California, and Orlando, Florida, were tied to immigrants.

UNDERSTANDING LEADS TO AWARENESS

In recent years, the increase in state measures aimed at cracking down on undocumented immigrants in the United States has also fueled anti-immigrant sentiment. As a result, many immigrants, and those who appear to be foreign born, have experienced more incidents of discrimination. For example, Arizona passed a controversial law in 2010 that required law enforcement officers to check the immigration status of everyone they encountered during a lawful stop, detention, or arrest if they had a reasonable suspicion that a person was undocumented. Opponents of the law protested that it encouraged police and community discrimination against immigrants. "A vastly disproportionate number of Hispanic Americans or Hispanic people in Arizona will be subjected to extra police intervention," said Jack Glaser, an associate professor of public policy at the University of California, Berkeley, in an article posted on the American Psychological Association website in September 2010, after the law's passage. "Even people who are completely legal, natural born citizens will now have a different existence in Arizona."

After several legal challenges to the law, Arizona announced in 2016 that police officers would no longer be required to demand immigration papers from people suspected of being undocumented.

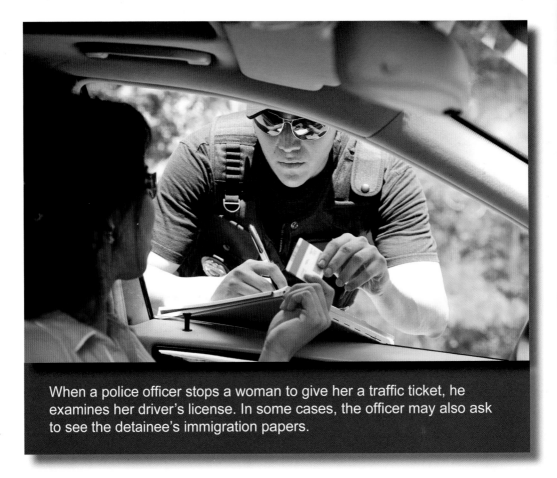

When a police officer stops a woman to give her a traffic ticket, he examines her driver's license. In some cases, the officer may also ask to see the detainee's immigration papers.

Understanding the history of discrimination against immigrants in the United States and how and why it occurs is the first step toward creating awareness. When people learn to recognize discrimination in their day-to-day lives, they can take measures to stand up, speak out, and safely confront it.

MYTHS AND FACTS

MYTH
Immigrants are overrunning the United States, and most are here illegally.

Fact
While there are more immigrants living in the United States than ever before, the percentage of immigrants in the overall population is very similar to the percentage at other times in history. In addition, the large majority of immigrants have lawful status.

MYTH
Most immigrants are violent criminals.

Fact
According to the Anti-Defamation League (ADL), immigrants are less likely than native-born citizens to commit crimes or become incarcerated.

MYTH
Immigrants are taking jobs from native-born Americans without paying taxes.

Fact
According to the ADL, immigrants help create new jobs by buying local products and starting their own businesses. States with large numbers of immigrants actually have lower unemployment rates. Also, studies have found that immigrants pay between $90 and $140 billion each year in taxes.

CHAPTER TWO

DISCRIMINATION AND THE LAW

Several laws prohibit discrimination based on national origin. This usually means treating people unfavorably because they are from a different country, because they appear to be of a certain ethnic background, or because they have an accent. National origin discrimination also occurs when a person married to or associated with an immigrant experiences unfavorable treatment, even when that person is native born. In some cases, discrimination occurs even when the victim and the person inflicting the discrimination are from the same country.

Immigration or citizenship-status discrimination is a related form of discrimination. It occurs when a person is treated unfavorably because of his or her citizenship or immigration status. It is based on the person's immigration status instead of whether the person or his or her ancestors came from another country. Like national-origin discrimination, immigration-status discrimination is against the law.

THE CIVIL RIGHTS ACT OF 1964

Several federal laws protect individuals from discrimination based on national origin or immigration status. The Civil Rights Act of 1964 outlaws discrimination on the basis of race, color, religion, sex, or national origin. It requires that all people be given equal access to public places, schools, and employment. One section of the act, called Title VII, specifically prohibits discrimination in the workplace based on race, sex, color, religion, and national origin. Title VII of the act applies to private employers, labor unions, and employment agencies. It outlaws discrimination in recruiting, hiring, wages, work assignments, promotions, benefits, discipline, firing, layoffs, and many other areas of employment.

In August 1963, civil rights protesters march in Washington, DC, to demand equal rights for African Americans, decent housing, integrated schools, and an end to segregation and bias.

In addition, Title VII of the Civil Rights Act of 1964 created the US Equal Employment Opportunity Commission (EEOC). The EEOC is a five-member commission that enforces federal anti-discrimination laws.

THE MESA SYSTEMS CASE

In 2013, Mesa Systems, Inc., a moving and storage company based in Grand Junction, Colorado, agreed to pay $450,000 to settle a national-origin discrimination lawsuit. According to the lawsuit, Hispanic workers at Mesa Systems' warehouse in Salt Lake City, Utah, experienced discrimination based on national origin. The immigrant employees faced a hostile work environment, including racist name-calling and slurs by the warehouse's managers. In addition, the warehouse had a restrictive language policy that negatively impacted employees of several national origins, including Hispanics, Asians, and Pacific Islanders. After submitting complaints to management, several employees were terminated or had their hours reduced. The lawsuit claimed that the company's actions violated Title VII of the Civil Rights Act of 1964.

In addition to the $450,000 settlement, the company agreed to several other actions, including adding discrimination training for employees, revising discriminatory policies, removing the restrictive language policy, and posting anti-discrimination notices at company facilities. EEOC Phoenix district director Rayford Irvin said in a September 2013 press release, "Offensive slurs and comments deriding one's national origin violate federal law and are never appropriate in the workplace. Employers need to ensure that this behavior is not allowed."

IMMIGRATION AND NATIONALITY ACT

The Immigration and Nationality Act (INA) is a federal law that covers many areas related to immigration. It has been amended several times over the years, including by the Immigration Reform and Control Act (IRCA) in 1986. The act protects people from employment discrimination based on national origin or immigration status. It makes it illegal to discriminate based on national origin or immigration status when hiring, firing, recruiting, or referring employees for a fee. The act also bans employers from demanding more or different documents to verify if a person is eligible for employment. It prohibits employers from refusing to accept documents offered by employees if they are legally acceptable and appear to be genuine. The act also bans intimidation, threats, coercion, or retaliation against a person who files charges or cooperates with an investigation under the act.

In 2011, the US Justice Department (DOJ) filed a lawsuit against Generations Healthcare (GHC), a company that runs assisted living facilities in California. The lawsuit claimed that GHC discriminated against foreign-born workers and violated the Immigration and Nationality Act. GHC required foreign-born employees to produce more documents to prove they were eligible to work than the company required of employees born in the United States. After an administrative court ruled with the Justice Department, GHC agreed to a settlement in 2014. The company will pay $119,313 in back pay to two discrimination victims and $88,687 in

In 2011, Generations Healthcare, a company that runs assisted living facilities in California, was accused of discriminating against foreign-born workers and violating the Immigration and Nationality Act.

civil penalties to the US government. The company will also have its hiring practices monitored for two years. "Both the court's ruling and this settlement underscore the importance of complying with the anti-discrimination provision of the Immigration and Nationality Act and the consequences for failing to do so," said Acting Assistant Attorney General Vanita Gupta for the Civil Rights Division in a December 2014 press release. "Employers should review their hiring policies and employment eligibility verification practices to ensure that they comply with federal anti-discrimination law."

PROMOTING DISCRIMINATION WITH THE LAW

Throughout US history, some laws and policies have the effect of promoting discrimination instead of preventing it. The Naturalization Act of 1790 restricted citizenship to free white men, excluding indentured servants, slaves, and American Indians. In 1882, President Chester A.

Chinese and white miners stand next to a sluice box in the Aubine Ravine in California in the 1850s. Many Chinese immigrants came to America to find work on the railroads or in mines.

(continued on the next page)

(continued from the previous page)

Arthur signed the Chinese Exclusion Act, which banned all immigration of Chinese laborers. In the 1920s, several laws sought to restrict the number of immigrants coming from southern and eastern Europe by imposing quotas. These quotas put annual restrictions on immigrants from European countries, while still excluding immigrants from Asian nations. It was not until 1965 that the national origins quota system was replaced in the Immigration and Nationality Act with a preference system that favored people reuniting with family and skilled immigrants. And in 1980, the Refugee Act created a way for refugees to apply for asylum in the United States for the first time. It also, however, set limits on refugees admitted to the country in order to prevent mass migrations.

FAIR HOUSING ACT

The Fair Housing Act bans discrimination that makes housing unavailable to a person because of his or her race, religion, gender, national origin, familial status, or disability. It applies to anyone involved in the housing process, including real estate agents, landlords, banks, mortgage companies, and insurance companies. This type of discrimination can be based on a person's country of birth or where his or her ancestors were born. In housing, examples of discrimination can occur if a rental agent tells an immigrant family there are no available apartments, even though apartments are being shown to American citizens. It also occurs when a realtor shows an immigrant family properties only in certain neighborhoods and refuses to show the family anything in other, nonimmigrant neighborhoods.

The Justice Department has taken action against some municipal governments that have tried to limit the number of Hispanic immigrant families living in their communities. They have sued lenders that have made home loans with less favorable terms for immigrant borrowers. And the DOJ has also taken action against landlords who have discriminated against immigrants from many areas of the world.

LEGAL RIGHTS OF UNDOCUMENTED IMMIGRANTS

Some federal laws apply only to citizens or nationals of the United States, permanent residents, lawful temporary residents, refugees, and people who have been granted political asylum. Under the United States Constitution, however, undocumented immigrants living and working in the United States do have some legal rights. These entitlements address certain basic human rights and apply to everyone in the country, even if they do not have the necessary immigration paperwork. The Fourteenth Amendment states that, "No state shall... deprive any person of life, liberty or property, without due process of law; nor deny to any person within its jurisdiction the equal protection of the laws." This means that undocumented immigrants have the right to a jury trial and the right to defend themselves against charges if arrested. If sued in civil court, the person has the right to be notified and defend themselves in court. Other amendments to the Constitution protect undocumented immigrants from unlawful search and seizure by law enforcement and against incriminating themselves. Undocumented immigrants also have the right to file lawsuits, including discrimination lawsuits, in federal court. In addition, some states have also granted various rights to undocumented immigrants, including the right to sue in state court.

Undocumented immigrants have the right to defend themselves against deportation from the United States. They have the right to a hearing before an immigration judge and representation by an attorney, although the US government does not have to pay for the lawyer.

Undocumented immigrants are also protected against discrimination based on race or nationality. Although employers must verify a person's legal authorization to live and work in the United States, they cannot single out certain employees because of their national origin or immigration status. They must ask for the same documentation from all employees.

EXECUTIVE ACTIONS FOR UNDOCUMENTED IMMIGRANTS

During his presidency, President Barack Obama signed two executive orders on undocumented immigration. In 2012, the Deferred Action for Childhood Arrivals (DACA) allowed young adults who had been brought to the United States as children without documentation to apply

President Barack Obama meets with a group of "DREAMers," children who were brought into the United States illegally and granted temporary relief under the 2012 DACA program.

for deportation relief and a temporary work permit. In 2014, President Obama signed the Deferred Action for Parents of Americans and Lawful Permanent Residents (DAPA). This action allowed some undocumented immigrants with children born in the United States to apply for deportation relief and a work permit. These policies were created to remove immigration enforcement and deportation efforts from undocumented immigrants who had been in the United States for many years and were law-abiding, contributing members of society.

AN INTENSE DEBATE

In recent years, immigration policies and laws have been a hotly debated topic around the country. Some people believe that the United States should relax its immigration restrictions and find a way to help millions of law-abiding undocumented immigrants become legal citizens. Others believe that current immigration laws and borders should be better enforced and protected.

During the 2016 election, US president Donald J. Trump made immigration reform a central issue of his campaign. After taking office in January 2017, Trump issued a series of executive orders reforming the United States' approach to enforcement of immigration policies. Many have questioned the legality of such orders.

CHAPTER THREE

RECOGNIZING AND REPORTING DISCRIMINATION

A lthough it is against the law, discrimination against immigrants still occurs in many schools, communities, and workplaces. Immigrants and their children may hear negative comments, slights, snubs, or slurs from community members. At stores and restaurants, they may receive poorer service, be treated with less respect, or treated as less intelligent or trustworthy than other customers. They may be denied safe and affordable housing. At school, they may be treated differently or given fewer opportunities. And at work, they may be denied employment, promotions, or paid less in wages simply because of their national origin or immigration status.

RECOGNIZING DISCRIMINATION IN SCHOOLS

For many young people, discrimination against immigrants in schools is one of their earliest experiences with this type of bias. Many foreign-born children or children of immigrant parents experience discrimination on a personal level, through the way schools and teachers treat them and the types of learning experiences offered them by their schools. Students may have negative interactions with teachers, school staff, and peers. This may include negative comments about their dress, appearance, and accent. Children report being insulted, called derogatory names, excluded from group activities, and being threatened and physically hurt by other students because they are immigrants. For example, one young Mexican immigrant says that a lot of kids in his class called him a beaner. "Personal discrimination may be direct, like racist comments or drawing attention to a child's personal appearance," Jennifer Adair, a

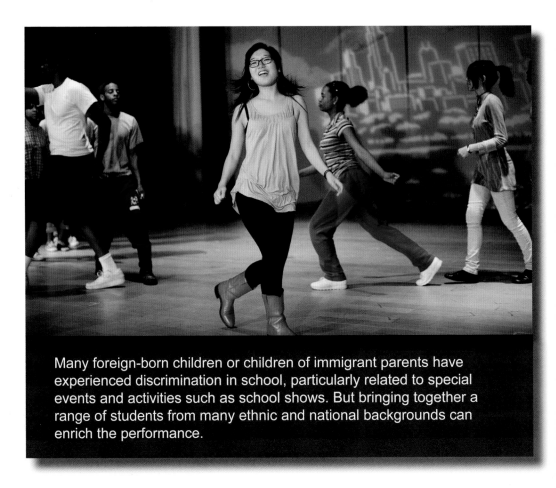

Many foreign-born children or children of immigrant parents have experienced discrimination in school, particularly related to special events and activities such as school shows. But bringing together a range of students from many ethnic and national backgrounds can enrich the performance.

professor at the University of Texas who has researched discriminatory attitudes toward young children from immigrant families in classrooms, said in a September 2015 article posted on Southern California Public Radio's website. She said indirect discrimination also occurs, "like questions about why their parents don't speak English or being asked to be the janitor or cleaner in a game instead of the princess or policeman." Adults can sometimes add to the problem, such as when teachers and staff become impatient with a student struggling to use English or administer tougher discipline to immigrant children as compared to other students.

DISCRIMINATION IN THE REAL WORLD

Learning how to recognize discrimination in its many forms and knowing to whom and how to report it is an important part of stopping discrimination altogether. Some examples of discrimination against immigrants in the real world include:

- A neighbor making comments that a teen's parents would have higher-paying jobs if they could speak English more fluently.
- An employer who does not hire a person because he or she only hires US citizens.
- An employer who asks for a prospective employee's work authorization papers but who has not asked other employees for similar paperwork.

(continued on the next page)

(continued from the previous page)

- An employer who does not hire a person because he or she doesn't want to deal with the hassle of filling out the necessary paperwork.
- A supervisor who insists on seeing a copy of an employee's green card after the employee has already provided a driver's license and social security card.
- A landlord who charges an immigrant higher rent than a native-born American.
- A bank that offers less favorable terms on a mortgage, such as a higher interest rate, because of a person's national origin or immigration status.
- Hotel staff who tell a guest that he or she must pay in cash instead of using a credit card and then charge the guest a higher rate than other customers and/or do not provide the guest with the same amenities that other guests get, such as towels and shampoo.
- A police officer who questions a foreign-born person and gets angry when the person does not speak English well enough to answer questions. The officer then arrests the person for disorderly conduct.

School staff may also have lower academic expectations for children of immigrants. Teachers may discourage immigrant children from signing up for advanced classes or not call on them to participate in class. If students are not fluent in English, teachers may overlook and underutilize other skills and talents the children might have. In addition, non-native English-speaking students are often placed in English as a Second Language (ESL) classes. In many ESL classrooms, inadequately qualified teachers or paraprofessionals mainly focus on English literacy, instead of other engaging educational material that builds creativity, problem-solving skills, and self-esteem. "Schooling for children of immigrants often begins by being labeled as not knowing something, not knowing English, not being ready for school—labels that are immediately negative and categorizing children as

Students raise their hands to answer a question during a class taught in Spanish in a bilingual elementary school in Texas. The students spend half their day learning in their native Spanish language and the other half learning in English.

deficient," said Adair. Instead of embracing a student's ability to speak a home language and English, some schools see it as a problem to be fixed.

Discrimination at school also occurs at an institutional or structural level. Many children of immigrants attend segregated schools—either by ethnicity, language, or income. According to a 2015 report from the Migration Policy Institute, nearly 25 percent of Texas schools have a majority of students who are Latino, English learners, and low income.

Schools in high-poverty areas, which are more likely to have children of immigrants, are often staffed by less-experienced and less-skilled teachers and staff. These schools have fewer resources available for students and are often overcrowded; students and teachers often have fewer opportunities to use technology. As a result, academic results are generally lower than average.

In addition, language barriers may prevent teachers from engaging with immigrant parents. Language barriers may also lead to misdiagnoses and placement in special education needs classes. Because many screening tests are conducted in English, they can incorrectly label a language learner as a student with a learning disability. Placed in special education classrooms, these students may not have access to appropriate learning opportunities.

UNDERSTANDING YOUR RIGHTS

Sometimes, discrimination because of national origin or immigration status goes unreported because victims do not understand their legal rights. Other times, victims may be afraid of retaliation if they report discrimination to the government. Therefore, it is critical that citizens and immigrants understand their legal rights and how to exercise them.

Everyone living in the United States has basic rights, including undocumented immigrants. If someone asks a person about his or her immigration status, that person has the right to remain silent. One does not have to answer questions about whether or not one is a US citizen, where he or she was born, or how he or she came to the country. If one has immigration papers, they should be shown to immigration agents if requested. Under no circumstances should one lie about citizenship status or hand over falsified documents.

If the police, immigration agents, or agents with the Federal Bureau of Investigation (FBI) come to your house, you should ask them why they are there. You may want to talk to the authorities through a closed door. If authorities do not speak your language, you can ask for an interpreter. If the authorities want to come inside, the occupant of the house should ask to see a warrant. This can be slid underneath the door. If authorities do not have a warrant issued by a court and signed by a judge, you do not have to let them into your home. If they have a warrant, the authorities can search only for the items listed on the warrant. An Immigration and Customs Enforcement (ICE) warrant does not give officers the right to enter a home without consent. Even if officers have a warrant, you still retain the right to remain silent. For more information, organizations like the American Civil Liberties Union (ACLU) provide fact sheets about rights as an immigrant and wallet cards with instructions on how to respond to law enforcement.

Officers from the immigrant removal task force of the Immigration and Customs Enforcement (ICE) stand outside a home during a raid to arrest and deport immigrants with deportation notices.

If you feel that your rights have been violated during any interactions with law enforcement or immigration officials, you should write down every memorable detail about the event, including the officer's badge and patrol car numbers. Find any witnesses and get their contact information. If there are any injuries, visit a doctor or hospital immediately and have them take pictures and document the injuries. Then you can file a complaint with the officer's internal affairs division or with a local civilian complaint board. In many cases, you may be able to file a complaint anonymously.

REPORTING DISCRIMINATION

Anyone who believes he or she has been a victim of discrimination because of national origin or immigration status can file a complaint. There are several agencies that deal with discrimination complaints, including the Department of Justice's Civil Rights Division, the Equal Employment Opportunity Commission (EEOC), and the office of Fair Housing and Equal Opportunity.

The Department of Justice's Civil Rights Division enforces civil rights laws, including those that pertain to discrimination based on national origin and immigration status. There are different divisions that handle different types of discrimination. The DOJ's website has information about the appropriate way to submit a complaint or report discrimination.

Everyone has the right to be treated fairly. Being able to recognize discrimination as it occurs in daily life can empower a person, whether he or she is a victim or a witness, to speak up and report it.

CHAPTER FOUR

WORKING TO END DISCRIMINATION

Throughout history, immigrant groups that were once discriminated against have been accepted into American society. Often this acceptance comes once people get to know and understand immigrants and realize their fears about them are unfounded. By working to understand each other, people can fight hate and discrimination and welcome people from all countries and backgrounds.

CONSEQUENCES OF DISCRIMINATION

Every day throughout the United States, immigrants encounter discrimination through insults, stereotypes, and lowered expectations at work, school, and in the community. In addition, millions of undocumented children and their families deal with social isolation, fear of detention and deportation, and the trauma of separation from family. These stressful experiences can have long-lasting negative effects.

Discrimination can have consequences on a person's health, emotions, behavior, education, and economic status. According to a 2015 report by the Migration

Policy Institute, immigrant children who encounter discrimination at school and in the community can develop depressive symptoms, anxiety, and low self-esteem. They may also become more likely to engage in aggressive and delinquent behavior. They may experience social isolation and feel as if they do not belong. And because teachers have low expectations, they are less likely to succeed at school and more likely to drop out of school altogether. Discrimination is especially harmful in a child's early years, when he or she is forming a sense of self. For adults and children, the physical and mental health effects of discrimination can cause increased absences from school and work.

For children and teens, separation from family members can also cause trauma. If a young child's undocumented parents are deported, the effect can be severe. These children often experience frequent bouts of crying, withdrawal from friends and family, disrupted eating and sleeping habits, anger, anxiety, and depression. In the long term, these effects can lead to more severe problems, such as posttraumatic stress disorder, difficulty forming relationships, acting out at school and home, and feelings of persecution.

STANDING UP FOR INCLUSION

Many people across the country are fighting hate and standing up for tolerance and inclusion. In February 2017, more than six hundred northern Virginia high school students from several schools walked out of class to show their support for immigrants and their rights. Rida Ali, a sixteen-year-old junior who helped organize the demonstration at Broad Run High School in Ashburn, Virginia, spoke to students at her school. "It's time to come together to outline the importance of diversity and immigration in our country. Immigrants are your teachers, your principals, your best friends, your government officials, your doctors, your neighbors," she said. In addition to organizing the student walkout, Ali and her mother volunteer for refugee causes and are preparing with their Maryland mosque to host a Syrian refugee family. "When you look around in your classrooms, there's so many people coming from so many different places," said Ali in a

Holding an American flag, Virginia high school student Rida Ali speaks to other students during a walkout she organized to show support for immigrants and their rights.

February 2017 article in the *Washington Post*. "Without immigration, everybody would be gone, unless you're Native American."

Other people are standing up against discrimination by helping to educate immigrants about their rights. Laura Melgarego works for PODER (People Organized to Demand Environmental and Economic Rights). Born in Mexico, Melgarego immigrated to the United States when she was fifteen years old. Today, she goes into communities and delivers education workshops in schools and churches that teach immigrant students and families about their rights and other immigration issues. "I care about this problem because I'm an immigrant myself and I know what it is like to experience discrimination," said Melgarego in a May 2014 interview posted on Missionlocal.org. "Also because the families that I work with experienced this every day, families feel that they do not have rights or cannot change what affects them. That is why I want to empower families by telling them that they have the rights."

TRAINING SCHOOL STAFF

Some schools are working to reduce discrimination and improve services for immigrant children and families. At the Family Life Academy Charter School in the Bronx, New York, teachers and school staff attend workshops throughout the year on how to work with immigrant

(continued on the next page)

(continued from the previous page)

A college student volunteers at Portland High School, helping several students who are English-language learners with their school assignments and learning the English language.

students who are learning the English language. More than 40 percent of the elementary school's students are classified as English language learners (ELL). All teachers receive training on how to meet the needs of ELL students, not just the ELL teachers. In addition, professional development sessions focus on topics such as the stages of language acquisition and classroom activities that can be used in each stage of a student's language development. Teachers and staff are encouraged to apply what they have learned to all students, not just ELL students.

BUILDING EMPATHY

One effective way to combat discrimination is to build empathy. Putting yourself in another person's shoes and seeing the world through his or her eyes can reduce bias and improve relationships with people from other countries and ethnic backgrounds. Teaching youth that subtle forms of discrimination such as ethnic slurs, stereotyping, and exclusion are hurtful can help prevent discrimination in the future.

According to David Levine, who leads empathy workshops at schools across the country, having empathy is more than just being nice. "The difference is the intention of reaching out to another person, the intention of bringing someone in to help them feel connected, to help them feel that they belong, to help them know that someone is really watching out for them and cares for them," he explained in a 2009 interview with NPR.org. Olivia Francis-Webber, a principal at Luis Llorens Torres Children's Academy in the Bronx, New York, has brought in Levine to present one of his workshops at her school. "Our school is made up of majority immigrants, from a variety of multicultural backgrounds. And they didn't understand each other's cultures and they tended to tease each other just… because of how they spoke, or how they looked, or their different habits," she said. After the workshops, Francis-Webber said that the number of fights and confrontations between students dropped significantly. Francis-Webber also said that many of her staff members, because they were not from the same cultural backgrounds as the students, also benefitted from Levine's empathy workshops.

In other schools, teachers are designing lessons to help all students develop empathy for each other and immigrant children. Some teachers have students interview their parents to learn how their own ancestors came to the United States and the difficulties they had to overcome. Then the students share what they have learned with classmates. Learning about the difficulties experienced by others, including some in their own families, helps students feel empathic toward classmates who are currently having similar experiences. At Grace Yokley Middle School in Ontario, California, teacher Dale Rosine worries about her students from immigrant families. "Some of the students from Mexico talk about the way they feel disrespected and second-rate in society," she said in a 2011 article posted on Tolerance.org. "They see what their parents go through, what lies ahead, and what's going to be available to them." To promote empathy and understanding, Rosine's class works on a family heritage project. The students conduct family research about their cultural heritage and the challenges they overcame. Some of her immigrant students talk about what it is like to come to a new country. Children of undocumented immigrants talk about their fears of being deported. Others recount how their families are separated in different countries. For many students, the project lowers walls and builds connections. "When they hear so many kids with different backgrounds and the difficulties they've had, it opens their eyes and makes their own situation seem less personal," she said. "They often remark that they thought they were the only ones who had experienced something until they heard their classmates' stories."

High school students from the Portland, Oregon, area participate in a diversity exercise during a Diversity Understanding Community Communication Conference, which discussed topics such as race, ethnicity, gender, and sexual orientation.

WHAT CAN I DO TO STOP DISCRIMINATION?

There are many ways that individuals can get involved to stop discrimination against immigrants. One of the best ways to get started is to take a look at your own life and challenge yourself to think and act in ways that are more inclusive and accepting. Don't laugh at offensive jokes or slurs. Think carefully about what language to use. Get to know people from different backgrounds and learn about their lives and hopes for the future.

Students can also combat discrimination by organizing awareness events at school. In 2016, students at the University of Oklahoma (OU) organized an informational event to support undocumented immigrants. The students set up booths on campus that provided information about avenues for direct action to support immigrant rights and held signs reading "No Human is Illegal." "We want to bring together people who care about the undocumented immigrants in our country," said senior Cooper Williams, the event's primary organizer, in a 2016 article posted on the university's website. Pamphlets offered instructions on how to respond to Immigration and Customs Enforcement officers and resources for low-cost legal services. "The goal for this event was to try to come up with ways for people to get involved, particularly locally," said senior Lena Wilson, an event organizer, in a 2017 article on the OU website. "For instance, there is a program that the Norman Public Library puts on where English speakers can tutor adults who are trying to learn English, and that can be really essential for someone trying to get a job or just participate socially in the community." Senior DeAndre Martin believes that events like these can build awareness and action. "Even if you touch just one person in these types of events, one person can save many," he said. "So I hope these continue to happen, and we can get away from all the racial things that are happening on campus and build a campus environment."

Students can talk to teachers and administrators about forming a human rights club at their school. Find a teacher who is willing to be the club's advisor and network with other teachers and students at

Protesters rally at Boston's Logan Airport to speak out against President Donald Trump's executive order to halt refugees and residents from predominantly Muslim countries from entering the United States.

other schools that have similar clubs. A human rights club allows students to engage in issues related to immigration and organize events for social change. The club can present examples of people and communities that are fighting for immigration rights around the world. Organizers might also explore working with other similar clubs, such as Amnesty International or a Model United Nations to see how they could work together. Through the club, students can take action through various activities, such as writing letters to government representatives, educating school students about issues, or organizing an event such as an immigrant rights march to bring awareness to immigrant issues.

CHAPTER FIVE

COPING WITH DISCRIMINATION

When experiencing discrimination, many people do not know what to do. A person may be upset and confused. He or she might want to tell someone but doesn't know whom to tell or where to start. There are many places for people who experience or witness discrimination based on national origin or immigration status to get help. Knowing where to go and whom to turn to is the first step toward coping.

Some people choose to report discrimination to the appropriate government agency. Others do not. It may take some time for a victim of discrimination to decide what he or she wants to do. The decision whether or not to report discrimination is entirely up to the victim. Some victims feel that reporting the discrimination will help them regain a sense of control and help them cope. Others choose not to report.

DISCRIMINATION AND STRESS

Discrimination can have a serious effect on a person's health. Being a target of discrimination can cause strong emotions to rise, such as anger, sadness, and embarrassment. These emotions can trigger a physical response, increasing a person's blood pressure, heart rate, and body temperature.

In addition, dealing with discrimination over time can lead to stress. According to the 2015 Stress in America survey, people who have experienced discrimination report higher stress levels on average than people who have not dealt with discrimination. Dealing with chronic stress can lead to a variety of physical and mental health issues. People who have chronic stress from discrimination are more likely to develop anxiety, depression, obesity, high blood pressure, and to abuse alcohol or drugs.

If you are struggling with depression, you may find it difficult to participate fully in your daily life. Depression is one of the health problems that can be triggered by chronic stress from dealing with discrimination.

Even if a person is not directly targeted by discrimination, just being a member of a group that is discriminated against can lead to higher stress levels. And worrying about discrimination creates more chronic stress in a person's life. A person who fears being in a situation where discrimination can occur may start avoiding these situations, missing out on social, educational, and job opportunities.

FOCUS ON STRENGTHS AND CHALLENGE NEGATIVE THOUGHTS

Because the stress of discrimination can have a negative effect on physical and mental health, finding healthy ways to cope is essential. One way to do this is to focus on individual strengths, values, and beliefs. Victims of discrimination often internalize the negative comments, slurs, and stereotypes they experience. They may begin to believe that they are not as good as other people. By concentrating on their strengths and positive attributes, a person may be better able to protect themselves against the negative effects of discrimination and prejudice. They can use their positive thoughts to banish negative beliefs and motivate themselves for success.

When people experience discrimination, some people may tell them to just shake it off and move on with their lives. This can be extremely difficult. Often, people spend time reliving and rehashing discriminatory events. Sometimes, this occurs because the person is not sure how to handle these events. A person may not know how to respond to discrimination or be afraid there will be retaliation, so he or she keeps thinking about the event and how he or she should have responded.

However, dwelling on negative thoughts and experiences can increase stress and anxiety. To stop this cycle of negativity, a person may want to talk with trusted family and friends about ways to handle similar experiences in the future. Having a plan can help a person stop dwelling on negative events in the past and feel confident in his or her ability to handle a similar situation in the future.

FIND SUPPORT SYSTEMS

Surrounding oneself with supportive people is another important part of coping with discrimination. Support

Finding a support group is a crucial step to coping with discrimination. Just receiving a hug and knowing that your friends are there, showing their support for you, can make a huge difference.

may come from family, friends, a therapist, or a group of people who have experienced a similar type of discrimination. Many people find that joining a support group and meeting others with similar experiences helps them better cope and relieve stress. Together, they can talk about discrimination and learn from each other about how to address and respond to different situations.

GETTING PROFESSIONAL HELP

Discrimination can be traumatic for many victims and is often difficult to manage. Some victims of discrimination find that therapy helps them better cope with feelings of stress and depression. Therapy aims to help people deal with challenges they are facing as they recover from traumatic experiences. In therapy, survivors can work through these feelings with a trained counselor. During a session, the survivor talks to a counselor about his or her feelings and problems and learns strategies to deal with them. Survivors learn coping skills, how to deal with feelings, and strategies to manage stress. They can also talk about thoughts and feelings that they are not comfortable discussing with friends and family.

There is no specific timeline for therapy. Treatment is meant to give a person the tools they need to deal with challenges and live their life in a healthy way. Some people accomplish their goals in a few months. Others find that they are more comfortable continuing to see their therapists for longer periods of time.

A support system can also be helpful if a person experiences discrimination in housing, employment, or education. That person can talk to other people about their experiences, which can help the victim of discrimination decide if he or she wants to report the discrimination to the appropriate authorities.

TAKING CARE OF ONESELF

Taking care of oneself is an important part of coping with discrimination. Eating well, exercising, and getting enough sleep are important to keep the body in balance. Exercise can fight feelings of stress, fatigue, and depression. Eating healthy and getting enough sleep helps the body feel good and function properly.

Emotional self-care is also critical for coping with discrimination. In addition to therapy, some people find that certain activities, such as art or writing, can help them express their thoughts and feelings and release stress. Some people find that meditation or yoga exercises release stress and promote a general sense of well-being.

Coping with discrimination takes time and effort. However, it is possible to manage one's responses and emotions. An important thing to remember about discrimination is that you are not alone. Help and support are available, and people are ready to speak up to end discrimination.

10 GREAT QUESTIONS
TO ASK AN IMMIGRATION LAWYER

1. Are you a member of the state bar association?

2. Are you a member of the American Immigration Lawyers Association (AILA)?

3. Does your office practice general law or do you specialize in immigration law?

4. How long have you been practicing law? What experience do you have with immigration and deportation cases?

5. What is your strategy for my case? What is the expected time frame?

6. Will any other lawyers or professionals in your office be working on the case?

7. What is the breakdown of costs for your services? What forms of payment do you accept, and do you have payment plans?

8. How long will it take to finish the work, and what are my chances of success?

9. Have you ever handled a case like mine, and what was the outcome?

10. When can you start working on my case?

GLOSSARY

ancestors The people from whom a person is descended.

discrimination Unfavorable treatment of another person based on race, gender, ethnic background, national origin, or other reasons.

exploit To use a situation or person unfairly.

green card A permanent resident card or proof that a person has the legal authorization to live and work in the United States.

immigrant A person who is born in one country and lives in another.

interpreter A person who translates another language, often verbally.

intolerance Unwillingness to accept views, beliefs, or behaviors that differ from one's own.

heritage Important traditions handed down from generation to generation.

microaggressions Intentional or unintentional slights, slurs, or insults used to demean another person.

national origin The country where a person was born.

native born Referring to a person born in the country in which he or she lives.

refugee A person who has been forced to leave his or her country in order to escape war, persecution, or natural disaster.

retaliation An action taken in revenge for filing a complaint or supporting another person's complaint.

slurs Comments that insult or demean another person.

stereotype An overly simple picture or opinion of a person, group, or thing.

terrorists People who use violence and threats to frighten people for a political goal.

FOR MORE INFORMATION

Canadian Council for Refugees
6839 Drolet Street, Suite 301
Montréal, QC H2S 2T1
Canada
(514) 277-7223
Website: http://ccrweb.ca/en
The Canadian Council for Refugees is a national nonprofit umbrella organization committed to the rights and protection of refugees and other vulnerable migrants in Canada and around the world and to the settlement of refugees and immigrants in Canada.

Equal Employment Opportunity Commission (EEOC)
31 M Street NE
Washington, DC 20507
(202) 663-4900
Website: http://www.eeoc.gov
Facebook: @USEEOC
Twitter: @useeoc
YouTube: @userTheEEOC
The US Equal Employment Opportunity Commission (EEOC) is a government agency that enforces federal discrimination laws. The EEOC enforces laws that make it illegal to discriminate against a job applicant or an employee because of the person's race, color, religion, sex (including pregnancy, gender identity, and sexual orientation), national origin, age (forty or older), disability, or genetic information. Information on filing a discrimination complaint can be found on the agency's website.

National Network for Immigrant and Refugee Rights
310 8th Street, Suite 310
Oakland, CA 94607
(510) 465-1984
Website: http://www.nnirr.org
Facebook: @nnirr
Twitter: @NNIRRnetwork
YouTube: @nnirr1985
The National Network for Immigrant and Refugee Rights
(NNIRR) works to defend and expand the rights of all
immigrants and refugees, regardless of immigration
status. Its website offers news articles, blog entries,
and information about ways to get involved in
advancing immigrant rights.

PEI Association for Newcomers to Canada
49 Water Street
Charlottetown, PE C1A 1A3
Canada
(902) 628-6009
Website: http://www.peianc.com
This nonprofit organization provides short-term
settlement services and long-term inclusion and
community integration programs for new immigrants
to Prince Edward Island in Canada. It also advocates
for immigrant issues.

United We Dream
1900 L Street NW, Suite 900
Washington, DC 20036
Website: http://unitedwedream.org
Facebook: @UnitedWeDream
Twitter: @unitedwedream

United We Dream is the largest immigrant youth-
led organization in the United States, made up of
about one hundred thousand immigrant youth. The
organization advocates for the fair treatment of
immigrants, regardless of their immigration status.

US Department of Housing and Urban Development
451 7th Street SW
Washington, DC 20410
(202) 708-1112
Website: http://www.hud.gov
Facebook: @HUD
Twitter: @hudgov
Instagram: @hudgov
YouTube: @HUDchannel
The US Department of Housing and Urban Development
oversees home ownership programs, low-income
housing assistance, fair housing laws, and other
housing-related issues. People who believe they have
been discriminated against in housing can file a
complaint with the department.

WEBSITES

Because of the changing nature of internet links, Rosen
Publishing has developed an online list of websites
related to the subject of this book. This site is updated
regularly. Please use this link to access this list:

http://www.rosenlinks.com/SPKUP/Immigrant

FOR FURTHER READING

Cruz, Barbara. *The Fight for Latino Civil Rights*. New York, NY: Enslow, 2016.

Howell, Sara. *Immigrants' Rights, Citizens' Rights*. New York, NY: PowerKids, 2015.

Hughes, Susan. *Making Canada Home: How Immigrants Shaped This Country*. Toronto, CA: Owlkids, 2016.

Lusted, Marcia Amidon. *Your Legal Rights as an Immigrant*. New York, NY: Rosen, 2016.

O'Donoghue, Sean. *The Disaster of the Irish Potato Famine: Irish Immigrants Arrive in America (1845–1850)*. New York, NY: PowerKids, 2016.

Osborne, Linda Barrett. *This Land Is Our Land: The History of American Immigration*. New York, NY: Abrams for Young Readers, 2016.

Pressberg, Dava. *Anti-Semitism: Jewish Immigrants Seek Safety in America (1881–1914)*. New York, NY: PowerKids, 2016.

Staley, Erin. *I'm an Undocumented Immigrant. Now What?* New York, NY: Rosen, 2017.

Warms, Ed. *Immigration to North America: Middle Eastern Immigrants*. Broomall, PA: Mason Crest, 2017.

Zoboi, Ibi Aanu. *American Street*. New York, NY: Balzer Bray, 2017.

BIBLIOGRAPHY

American Civil Liberties Union. "Know Your Rights: What to Do If Immigration Agents (ICE) Are At Your Door." ACLU. Retrieved June 5, 2017. http://www.aclu.org/know-your -rights/what-do-if-immigration-agents-ice-are-your-door.

American Immigration Council. "How the United States Immigration System Works." American Immigration Council Fact Sheet, August 12, 2016. https://www .americanimmigrationcouncil.org/research/how-united -states-immigration-system-works.

Balingit, Moriah. "Hundreds of Virginia High School Students Walk out in Support of Immigrants." *Washington Post*, February 10, 2017. https://www.washingtonpost.com/ local/education/students-at-virginia-high-schools-plan -walkout-friday-in-support-of-immigrants /2017/02/10/27ed1072-efae-11e6-9973 -c5efb7ccfb0d_story.html?utm_term=.dd4916a40965.

Branch, Kayla. "OU Students Organize Informational Event in Support of Undocumented Immigrants." *OU Daily*, November 18, 2016. http://www.oudaily.com/news /ou-students-organize-informational-event-in-support -of-undocumented-immigrants/article_8ab74962-adcc -11e6-ac93-1736bc0c5ab4.html.

Costello, Maureen. "The Face of Human Immigration." *Teaching Tolerance*, Spring 2011, Number 39. http:// www.tolerance.org/magazine/number-39-spring-2011 /feature/human-face-immigration.

Fernandes, Deepa. "Discrimination Begins Early and Immigrant Preschoolers Notice, Report Says." Southern California Public Radio, September 14, 2015. http:// www.scpr.org/news/2015/09/14/54355 /discrimination-begins-early-and-immigrant-preschoo.

Holohan, Meghan. "High School Club Aims to Make Refugees, Immigrants Welcome." Today.com. March 2, 2017. http://www.today.com/parents/high-school-club-aims-make-refugees-immigrants-welcome-t108229.

Munsey, Christopher. "Deciding Who Belongs." American Psychological Association. September 2010. http://www.apa.org/monitor/2010/09/immigration.aspx.

National Archives. "The Civil Rights Act of 1964 and the Equal Employment Opportunity Commission." October 9, 2016. https://www.archives.gov/education/lessons/civil-rights-act.

National Immigration Law Center. https://www.nilc.org.

NPR.org. "Educators Fight Violence with Empathy." NPR Education, April 20, 2009. http://www.npr.org/templates/story/story.php?storyId=103274911.

Office of Public Affairs. "Justice Department Settles Lawsuit Against California Employer Over Discrimination Against Foreign-Born Workers." Department of Justice. December 14, 2014. https://www.justice.gov/opa/pr/justice-department-settles-lawsuit-against-california-employer-over-discrimination-against.

Pew Research Center. http://www.pewresearch.org/topics/immigration.

Students from the San Francisco International High School. "Fighting Immigrant Discrimination." Mission Local, May 14, 2014. https://missionlocal.org/2014/05/fighting-immigrant-discrimination.

US Equal Employment Opportunity Commission. "Mesa Systems to Pay $450,000 to Settle EEOC National Origin Discrimination Lawsuit." US Equal Employment Opportunity Commission Press Release. September 30, 2013. https://www.eeoc.gov/eeoc/newsroom/release/9-30-13a.cfm.

INDEX

ABOUT THE AUTHOR

Carla Mooney is a graduate of the University of Pennsylvania. She writes for young people and is the author of many books for young adults and children. Mooney enjoys learning about social issues and making the world a more inclusive place for all people.

PHOTO CREDITS